AMAZING GARDENS
OF THE WORLD

AMAZING GARDENS
OF THE WORLD

SPECTACULAR CLASSIC & CONTEMPORARY GARDENS

Vivienne Hambly

amber
BOOKS

Published by Amber Books Ltd
United House
North Road
London N7 9DP
United Kingdom
www.amberbooks.co.uk
Instagram: amberbooksltd
Facebook: amberbooks
Twitter: @amberbooks
Pinterest: amberbooksltd

ISBN: 978-1-83886-198-8

Project Editor: Michael Spilling
Designer: Mark Batley
Picture Research: Terry Forshaw

Printed in China

Contents

Introduction

Gardening today rests on traditions built up over millennia. Our first attempts at ornamental horticulture began in the Fertile Crescent, the productive lands stretching from the Tigris and Euphrates in modern-day Iraq and Syria, to the Nile in Egypt. Here, nutrient-rich soils and reliable water supply meant populations could not only settle but establish the social hierarchies that permitted decorative cultivation. Since then, gardens and gardening have come to represent as many interests as there are places in the world. Religious symbolism is innate to

many gardens in the Far East. Medicinal plants inspired the first European botanic gardens. Monarchs built gardens to display wealth or to trump rivals. Invading forces, whether Roman, Norman, Mughal or British, established gardens in statements of strength and acquisition. Still other gardens are outlets for creative energy, offer respite from personal difficulty or provide escape from the humdrum of life. Meanwhile, the most forward-looking gardens have sustainability and biodiversity at their heart.

ABOVE:
Royal Botanic Gardens, Kew, England
These gardens in southwest London date from 1759, when Princess Augusta, the mother of King George III established botanic garden within her pleasure grounds. Today, RBG Kew is at the forefront of botanical research.

OPPOSITE:
Tirta Gangga, Bali, Indonesia
In east Bali, this water garden was built by the Karangasem royal family in 1948. Volcanic activity interrupted construction, which resumed in the 1960s. It comprises three levels featuring fountains and decorative ponds.

Europe

It is difficult to overstate the influence of this diverse, densely populated continent on botanical tradition around the world. In 1758 in Sweden, Carl Linnaeus developed binomial nomenclature, a system of categorising plants that has come to be used in all spheres of formal horticulture and botany, often at the cost of indigenous knowledge. From Europe's courts and palaces were planned invasions on opposite sides of the globe. Colonial settlers introduced European patterns of gardening to their host countries. If commercial crops such as cocoa, tea and coffee were not being moved from colony to colony, specimen plants were returned by plant hunter-explorers to private nurseries and botanic gardens for collection. It is also impossible to ignore the fact that many great gardens were built with the spoils of the slave trade. For all this, Europe's gardens are by and large the finest in the world. They reflect the continent's creative life, the entangled, often brutal nature of its politics, and have led to extraordinary scientific innovation. Botanical gardens once established to further medicinal knowledge are now at the forefront of global conservation efforts, and they continue to aid the search for cures to our deadliest diseases. The artificial lakes of the English landscape movement, emulated across Europe, were the forerunners of canal transport systems. Expansive glasshouses which were often built to accommodate the influx of exotic plants from around the world, whether palms or pineapples, laid the foundations of modern skyscrapers. Artists like Derek Jarman fashioned intensely personal gardens from unlikely circumstances, while Louis XIV's Palace of Versailles was so extravagant, so ornate, it was envied from St Petersburg to Rome.

OPPOSITE:
Château de Villandry, Indre-et-Loire, France
Archeologists have dated some work at Château de Villandry to 1532. Its current incarnation is the much more recent vision of Joachim Carvallo, who, having restored the building in the 1900s, implemented the opulent Renaissance-style planting we see today.

LEFT & ABOVE:

**Crathes Castle,
Aberdeenshire, Scotland**
Now in the care of the
National Trust for Scotland,
16th-century Crathes Castle
was for 350 years the home
of the Burnett family. In the
early 20th-century walled
garden built by Sir James
Burnett and his wife Sybill,
roses and herbaceous borders
abound. Some yew planting
here, in topiary and hedging,
is believed to date from 1702.

OVERLEAF:

**Royal Botanic Garden
Edinburgh, Scotland**
Like many early gardens, the
function of the RBGE was
practical: it was founded
in 1670 with the express
purpose of supplying plants
for study and medical
treatment. Now 300 years
old, its scope is wide-ranging
and global, with energies
directed towards education,
conservation and science
programmes.

LEFT:

Frederiksborg Castle, Hovedstaden, Denmark
An example of early 17th-century architecture, Frederiksborg Castle was built by King Christian IV between 1600 and 1621 and named for his father, Frederick. In the Baroque garden, around 65,000 box trees shape the monograms of certain royals. By contrast, the informal Landscape garden is typical of this 19th-century style, with paths, canals and shrubberies contriving to make a 'natural' landscape.

RIGHT & OVERLEAF:

Hampton Court Palace, Surrey, England
The home of England's most notorious king, Henry VIII, this magnificent palace on the banks of the river Thames is surrounded by 24ha (60 acres) of formal garden and a further 303ha (750 acres) of parkland. Garden highlights include the restored Baroque-style Privy Garden, Kitchen Garden and the world's oldest puzzle maze, dating from around 1700.

ALL PHOTOGRAPHS:
Forde Abbey, Dorset, England

In the gentle hills of southern England, Forde Abbey is a former Cistercian retreat with a garden 900 years in the making. While the Great Pond is the only remaining monastic element, successive generations have shaped the garden here. New features include a floral labyrinth and meadow planting.

ALL PHOTOGRAPHS:

Great Dixter, East Sussex, England

Sir Edwin Lutyens made additions to this 15th century building and garden in the early 20th century, but it is the gardener and gardening writer Christopher Lloyd (1921–2006) who put his family home on the map. The spirit of Lloyd's colourful, inventive planting combined with quirky topiary is now maintained by Fergus Garrett and the Great Dixter Charitable Trust. Influential through its learning programmes, the garden has gathered legions of fans around the world.

ALL PHOTOGRAPHS:
Hatfield House, Hertfordshire, England

This Jacobean house 21 miles north of London, was built in 1611 by first Earl of Salisbury Robert Cecil, although it is based on an older palace, in which Elizabeth I learned she would be Queen. The house has remained the property of the Cecil family ever since. Highlights include parterres in the East Garden, a maze, yew hedges and topiary, and a walk of pleached lime trees.

Tresco Abbey Gardens, Isles of Scilly, England
Tresco is one of five inhabited islands in Isles of Scilly archipelago, 28 miles southwest of Cornwall. Here the subtropical Tresco Abbey Gardens, warmed by the effects of the Gulf Stream, were established around the ruins of a Benedictine abbey in the 18th century. Around 20,000 subtropical plants thrive in what must be one of the most picturesque gardens in the world.

ALL PHOTOGRAPHS:

Blenheim Palace, Oxfordshire, England

The seat of the Dukes of Marlborough since 1704, this UNESCO World Heritage Site is the only non-royal, non-episcopal palace in the country. The land for the palace was given to the first Duke of Marlborough following his success at the Battle of Blenheim (1704). In recent decades, it has become known for being the birthplace of Sir Winston Churchill.

Sir Lancelot 'Capability' Brown designed a substantial landscape park in 1764. Formal gardens surrounding the palace (above) feature water terraces, a rose garden and an Italian garden. Beyond, the Walled Garden houses a three-kilometre (two-mile) long yew maze.

ALL PHOTOGRAPHS:

Trebah, Cornwall, England
Some 10.5ha (26 acres) make
up the subtropical gardens of
this Cornish property on the
river Helford, near Falmouth.
It was established in 1831
by Charles Fox and latterly
restored by Tony Hibbert.
The mild climate and acidic
soil provide ideal conditions
for 140-year-old rhodendrons,
magnolias, camellias and
hydrangeas, which thrive here.

Polgwidden beach, at the
foot of the gardens, was used
to launch the World War II
offensive on Omaha Beach in
Normandy, France.

Prospect Cottage, Kent, England

It is arguable that the greatest work of Derek Jarman (1942–1994) was not film-making for which he was known, but the post-modern garden he created on a shingle spit beside Dungeness nuclear power station. Buying a former fisherman's cottage in 1984, Jarman fashioned the garden from flotsam, shingle and hardy plants. It would later provide the inspiration for Beth Chatto's renowned gravel garden at her property near Chelmsford, Essex. In 2020, the cottage, at risk of falling into private ownership, was bought for the nation thanks to a £3.5 million fund-raising campaign.

ALL PHOTOGRAPHS:

Sissinghurst Castle Garden, Kent, England
Few gardens in the world enjoy the popularity of Sissinghurst, the life's work of Vita Sackville-West and Harold Nicholson, who bought the Tudor property in 1930. The White Garden, in particular, has inspired amateur gardeners for decades. The property is now in care of the National Trust and in 2021, a dry-climate garden based on Harold and Vita's travels to the Greek island of Delos was opened.

ALL PHOTOGRAPHS:
Stourhead, Wiltshire, England
The property of the Stourton family for half a century, Stourhead came into the possession of the Hoares, the banking family, in 1717. The house, one of England's greatest Palladian mansions, remained in the family until 1949, when it was given to the National Trust. The surrounding mid-18th century gardens are in the English landscape style with an artificial lake and views framed by classical follies and monuments.

OPPOSITE:

Arundel Castle, West Sussex, England

Positioned on a hill in the pretty village of Arundel, this castle dates to 1067 and Charles de Montgomery, first holder of the earldom of Arundel which was given to him by William the Conqueror. The densely arranged gardens, which include substantial glasshouses, are packed with spring bulbs, while the Rose Garden comes to the fore in summer. Opened in 2008, the Collector Earl's garden, containing a pergola and central canal, is a memorial to the 14th Earl of Arundel.

ALL PHOTOGRAPHS RIGHT:

Chelsea Physic Garden, London, England

Beside the banks of the river Thames, central London, the four-acre Chelsea Physic Garden has been the site of medicinal plant growing since 1673. Use of property was secured in 1712 by Sir Hans Sloane and the garden continues to pay an annual rent of £5 to his descendants.

On his travels to the West Indies, Sloane had noticed Jamaicans drinking cocoa with water to settle the stomach. A renowned physician, Sloane adapted their recipe, which led the Cadbury brothers to sell drinking chocolate under his name. Today around 5,000 edible and medicinal plants feature in this green space.

ALL PHOTOGRAPHS:

Royal Botanic Gardens, Kew, Surrey, England
Possibly the greatest garden in the world, RBG Kew was formally opened in 1840, although it had been operating from its site in southwest London from at least 1759. Much of the garden's original work was to source plants with commercial potential from new territories, relying on the endeavours of robust plant-hunter explorers. Such activities gathered pace under the first director, William Hooker.

The plant titan arum (*Amorphophallus titanum*) is famed for smelling of rotting flesh when it flowers (right). It is housed in the Princess of Wales Conservatory.

LEFT:

Royal Botanic Gardens, Kew, Surrey, England
While reckoning with its imperial past, the current focus of RBG Kew is broadly on conservation and maintaining biodiversity. The Millenium Seed Bank at the gardens' second site, Wakehurst, holds in secure conditions seeds of roughly 39,000 species from around world.

OVERLEAF (BOTH PHOTOGRAPHS):

Eden Project, Cornwall, England
Two unmistakable geodesic domes filled with plant specimens from around the world form the backbone of the Eden Project in Cornwall. The brainchild of Sir Tim Smit, the garden grew out of an old quarry site, took two-and-a-half years to build, and opened formally in 2001. While there is plenty of outdoor planting, tropical and Mediterranean biomes are housed beneath the domes. Rainwater harvesting and green energy strategies put sustainability at the heart of the garden.

41

ALL PHOTOGRAPHS:

Lost Gardens of Heligan, Cornwall, England
After World War I took the lives of many gardeners who went to fight in the trenches, the gardens at Heligan were left to ruin, to be reclaimed only in the 1990s by Sir Tim Smit. By that time, they were so overgrown, metal detectors were used to locate old tools and greenhouse parts. While the Walled Garden here is an exercise in immaculate productive gardening, steeply sloping wilder sections include the Jungle and the Lost Valley which are planted with gunnera and tree ferns.

ALL PHOTOGRAPHS:
Levens Hall, North Yorkshire, England
Quirky topiary forms, both abstract and geometric, are a hallmark of this garden dating from the 1690s. The clipped yew and box shapes constitute what is believed to be the world's oldest topiary garden. Herbaceous borders, lawns, roses and a productive garden complete the scene.

Powerscourt, County Wicklow, Ireland
Although Powerscourt dates from 1731, the 19ha (47-acre) gardens here were developed chiefly in the 19th century. They are expansive and include a Japanese garden, lake, walled garden and a pet cemetery. The property is owned by members of the Slazenger family, who were once makers of sporting goods.

PREVIOUS PAGES, LEFT & RIGHT:
**Palace de Versailles,
Île-de-France, France**
Louis XIV placed as much
emphasis on the gardens at
the Palace of Versailles as he
did the building. In 1661, he
instructed André Le Nôtre to
create, over four decades, what
would become one of the
world's most admired gardens.
The intensely formal designs
include parterres, clipped
hedging, fountains and canals.
Aspects of this UNESCO
World Heritage Site were
replanted in the early part of
this century.

ALL PHOTOGRAPHS:
**Château de Villandry,
Indre-et-Loire, France**
In the gardens of the
Renaissance-era Château de
Villandry, organic productive
spaces are among the most
exceptional. In autumn,
decorative cabbages jostle
with leeks, late tomatoes,
kale and squash. These
particular spaces are the
vision of Joachim Carvallo
and his American wife
Anne Coleman, great-
grandparents of the current
owner, Henri Carvallo.

ALL PHOTOGRAPHS:

**Château de Villandry,
Indre-et-Loire, France**
The gardens here date to the
construction of the château
in 1532, with archaeologists
revealing the presence of a
decorative kitchen garden
near the house. Around the
18th century, the grounds
were designed in the style
of an English park, in
the style promulgated by
'Capability' Brown, Humphry
Repton and William Kent,
particularly. In the early
1900s, having restored the
château to its Renaissance
splendour, Carallo ordered the
Renaissance arrangements we
see today.

PREVIOUS PAGES AND RIGHT:
Monet's Garden at Giverny, Eure, France
This most famous painter's garden, begun in the 1880s, is a garden of two parts. Its Japanese water garden, some distance from the house, was inspired by prints the painter collected and it was later immortalised in his paintings. The second garden, close to the house, focuses on symmetry and perspective achieved through flower beds, fruit trees and climbing roses.

ALL PHOTOGRAPHS:

Villa Ephrussi de Rothschild, Alpes-Maritimes, France

Between glamorous Nice and Monaco, on the promontory of Saint-Jean-Cap-Ferrat, Villa Ephrussi de Rothschild is the vision of Baroness Beatrice de Rothschild (1864–1934), who imagined the main garden in the shape of a ship's deck. Built from 1907–12, the organic garden comprises eight themed rooms, including French, Spanish, Japanese, Provençal and Florentine. The captivating garden has been classified as one of the Remarkable Gardens of France.

ALL PHOTOGRAPHS:
Jardin Exotique, Monaco
In 1933, the Exotic Garden of Monaco was built into a cliffside overlooking the Mediterranean. A botanical garden, its striking setting is the ideal location for collections of succulents and cacti gathered from around the world. These collections were started as early as 1865.

Keukenhof, Lisse, Netherlands

Without doubt, Keukenhof offers the most admired display of spring bulbs in the world. Each year, from March to May, around seven million bulbs come into flower in the 200ha (494-acre) park, in what is now one of Europe's key tourist attractions. Although the garden dates to the 15th century and Countess Jacoba van Beieren, the displays we see today began as recently as 1949, when a group of 20 bulb specialists thought to put on a spring display.

67

ALL PHOTOGRAPHS:

Keukenhof, Lisse, Netherlands
Now described as a living catalogue of the work of 100 bulb breeders, Keukenhof reflects the bulb and cut-flower growing heritage of this country, which reached its infamous peak in the tulipmania of the 17th century. Around 500 growers of cut-flowers also take part in nearly two dozen flower shows here.

Herrenhausen Palace, Lower Saxony, Germany
Britain's centuries-old links with Europe become apparent at Schloss Herrenhausen, Hanover, erstwhile palace of King George II and King George III, who also held the Duchy of Brunswick-Lüneburg. It was in fact an heir to the British throne, Sophia of Hanover, who initiated the construction of these grand palace gardens in 1683. The Great Garden here epitomises Baroque style and is unchanged from its 300-year-old plan. Other gardens are designed in the English landscape style.

LEFT:

Schwerin Castle, Mecklenburg-Vorpommern, Germany
Some kind of fortification has existed on the site of Schwerin castle for at least the past millennium. The current building was constructed around an older structure in the mid-1800s, for Friedrich Franz II, Grand Duke of Mecklenburg-Schwerin, although the castle is now a public building. The island location in the city of Schwerin must be one of the most romantic imaginable. Baroque features date from 1748, with newer elements introduced in the 1800s.

OVERLEAF:

Sanssouci Palace and Park, Brandenburg, Germany
This UNESCO World Heritage Site was built between 1745 and 1747. Sansscouci translates literally as 'without a care', and it was the name Friedrich the Great, King of Prussia, gave to this summer palace in the city of Potsdam.

ALL PHOTOGRAPHS:

Sanssouci Palace and Park, Brandenburg, Germany
Formal terraces lead down from the palace to the Baroque-style garden designed in the 19th century by Peter Joseph Lenné. The expansive grounds include such features as a grotto, neoclassical temples, a large fountain and a Chinese house, incorporating rococo and chinoiserie elements. The last attraction to be built here was the Orangery Palace, ordered by Wilhelm IV. This handsome building is an ideal place for overwintering tender plants.

ALL PHOTOGRAPHS:

Mirabell Palace and Gardens, Salzburg, Austria

Sharp-eyed fans of *The Sound of Music* will recognize the Pegasus Fountain in Salzburg's Mirabell Palace gardens: it is where Judy Garland, as Maria, and the children danced and sang 'Do Re Mi' in the 1965 film. This Salzburg landmark was built in 1606 but the gardens that we see were laid out in 1690. Classically Baroque in style, they include a rose garden fountain, orangery and hedge theatre.

Volksgarten, Vienna, Austria

This public park in Austria's only metropolitan city was laid out in 1821 by Ludwig Remy and opened to the public in 1823. Volksgarten translates as 'people's garden', reflecting the fact that it was built over city fortifications destroyed by Napoleon in 1809. In time, other fortifications which were no longer needed were removed and the park was expanded. The public space became so popular that Johann Strauss I even wrote a piece entitled Volksgarten Quadrille.

ALL PHOTOGRAPHS:
Zagreb Botanical Garden, Croatia
Laid out in 1890, this botanical garden is attached to the
Faculty of Science at Zagreb University. It contains around
5,000 different specimens, and has a particular focus on
preserving native flora. Within the 2ha (5-acre) garden in the
heart of the city, find flower parterres, glasshouses, a rock
garden and an arboretum in the English landscape style.

LEFT:

Caserta Royal Palace and Park, Campania, Italy
Drawing heavily from Versailles and covering 4ha (9.8 acres), the UNESCO World Heritage Site outside Naples comprises fountains, pools and cascades, in what UNESCO describes as 'a triumph of Italian Baroque'. It was built for Charles III, King of Naples and Italy and later King of Spain, by Luigi Vanvitelli. A later English landscape garden was designed for Queen Maria Carolina, sister of Marie Antoinette, by John Andreas Graefer.

RIGHT:

La Venaria Reale, Piedmont, Italy
This Baroque palace near Turin was built for the Royal House of Savoy in the 17th and 18th centuries, but by the 20th it had fallen to ruin. An extensive restoration programme now puts this UNESCO World Heritage Site on the map. The gardens offer 80ha (200 acres) of Baroque splendour, including terraces, sculptures, canals and the largest potager in Italy.

ALL PHOTOGRAPHS:
Villa d'Este, Lazio, Italy
One of the most famous gardens of all, Villa d'Este in Tivoli is a superb example of Renaissance design and has provided the pattern for many subsequent garden designs. The UNESCO World Heritage Site was laid out by Pirro Ligorio, for Cardinal Ippolito II d'Este of Ferrara in the mid-16th century. Two slopes descend to a terrace in which water features heavily. The Fountain of Organ is an early feat of engineering.

ALL PHOTOGRAPHS:

Orto Botanico di Padova, Veneto, Italy

Although the botanic garden in Pisa pips this garden by a year, the botanic garden of Padua, founded in 1545, and has never moved from its site, putting it in the running for oldest botanic garden in the world. It was initiated by the Senate of the Venetian Republic as a place where medicinal plants could be studied. Today it is a UNESCO World Heritage Site.

ALL PHOTOGRAPHS:

Quinta da Regaleira, Lisbon, Portugal
In the wooded hills above Lisbon, the village of Sintra is the site of a number of remarkable gardens. Key among them is this palace, the 4ha (9.8-acre) grounds of which are a confection of grottoes, wells, fountains and lakes built for Carvalho Monteiro in the late 19th century by Luigi Manini, an Italian architect. The complex is a UNESCO World Heritage Site.

ALL PHOTOGRAPHS:

Alhambra, Granada, Spain

The influence of Islamic garden spans north India to Spain, where in Granada the Alhambra is one of the most exalted gardens in the world. Positioned on a rocky hill, the palace was built in the 13th century by Muhammad I of Granada, also known as Ibn al-Ahmar. By the 14th century, various rooms had been built for successive rulers, but as with so many Islamic gardens, water as well as containment and exposure are key features here.

Alhambra, Granada, Spain
Columns, passages and courtyards offer a sublime visitor experience. Sections of the gardens include the Court of the Myrtiles and the Court of the Lions, which was built for Muhammad V and takes the form of the iconic Islamic chahar bagh, a square divided into four, with a central water feature. It is a UNESCO World Heritage Site.

OVERLEAF:

Topkapi Palace, Istanbul, Turkey
In Istanbul, overlooking the Bosphorus and the Sea of Marmara, the Ottoman sultan Mehmed the Conqueror built a large garden to cement his presence in the region. The gardens here are a sequence of interlinking rooms, housed within a much larger garden periphery. As in all Islamic gardens, water features prominently.

LEFT & RIGHT:

Peterhof Palace, St Petersburg, Russia

A range of gardens styles prevails at this notable palace in St Petersburg, which has won acclaim for its 64 fountains, terraces and cascades richly symbolic of Russian might. The garden was ordered by Peter the Great in the 18th century, who wished for his palace to rival Versailles – he went as far as appointing Jean-Baptiste Alexandre Le Blond, a contemporary of Versailles designer André Le Nôtre.

Inevitably for such a great garden, Peterhof has seen its fortunes fluctuate over centuries. It was raided by German forces in World War II, when the palace was captured and left to burn. The fountains were ruined and fighting took place in the Lower Gardens. Extensive restoration projects have brought this property back to life and the site marked its 300th anniversary in 2003.

OVERLEAF:

Kadriorg Palace, Tallinn, Estonia

After capturing Tallinn in 1710, Peter the Great ordered Kadriog Palace for his wife, Catherine, and work began on it in 1718. It was little used, however, and much of what we see today is the 19th century vision of Nicholas I of Russia. Baroque planting was restored in the late 1990s.

Africa and the Middle East

For much of Africa, the act of survival defines what may be grown. In the north, where resources are scant, the Berbers or Amazighs must be nomadic to live. South of the Sahara, all the way down to the Nguni tribes of southern Africa, subsistence farmers hold up the continent, with rare capacity for ornamental gardening. Yet, where ornamental gardens do exist, they are magnificent, often reflecting the colonial powers that scrambled for this resource-rich continent. In Morocco, the French painter Jacques Majorelle was so taken with the colours used by the Amazigh around him, that he splashed cobalt blue across walls and fountains to create a compelling spectacle of a garden in this arid country. The tropical islands of Mauritius and the Seychelles saw both French and British rule which is echoed in their long-established botanic gardens. On the very tip of the continent, the first white settler at the Cape of Good Hope, now Cape Town, Jan van Riebeeck, planted a defensive hedge on a farm in 1660. In what is now Kirstenbosch National Botanical Garden a remnant remains, but far more striking today is a Camphor Avenue planted by the British in 1898.

Arab influences have trickled into East Africa for centuries but it is in the Middle East itself that the classic Islamic garden, the chahar bagh, is most pronounced. In Iran, on the banks of the River Koshk, the Bagh-e Eram takes its name from what we can only dream of: paradise.

OPPOSITE:
Jardin Majorelle, Marrakesh-Safi, Morocco
In Marrakesh, this extraordinary garden, one of the most striking and best-known in Africa, was originally the work of French painter Jacques Majorelle. The artist began work here in 1924 and painted walls, fountains and rills in a distinctive cobalt blue he had seen used in Amazigh or Berber communities.

ALL PHOTOGRAPHS:
**Jardin Majorelle,
Marrakesh-Safi, Morocco**
The garden was bought in 1980 by fashion designer Yves Saint Laurent and Pierre Bergé, his partner. Their intention was to restore the property, which had fallen into neglect after Majorelle's divorce in the 1950s and death in 1963. The Musée Berbère is at the heart of the garden and contains Amazigh artefacts initially collected by Majorelle. In 2017, a further museum housing the items from the collection of Yves Saint Laurent and Pierre Bergé was opened. The ashes of Laurent, who died in 2008, are scattered in the garden.

Jardin Majorelle, Marrakesh-Safi, Morocco
In addition to painting, Marjorelle was also a keen plant collector and spent decades working on the garden. Water, whether in fountains, furrows or rills is dominant here, in echoes of traditional Islamic gardens. There is a fine collection of cacti, while bamboos, succulents and palms add to the mood of the property.

ALL PHOTOGRAPHS:

El-Hamma Botanical Garden, Algiers, Algeria
Fashioned from drained ground in the Bay of Algiers in 1832, this 32ha (79-acre) botanical garden carries the influences of its French and English colonial powers. Bougainvilleas and palm trees create lush vistas here, and a broad walk affords views down to the sea. Initially used as a trial garden, it is today a popular public park.

ALL PHOTOGRAPHS:

**Aswan Botanical Garden,
Aswan, Egypt**

A striking backdrop of sand dunes defines the Aswan Botanical Garden, which occupies the entire El Nabatat Island, on the river Nile. The island was once in the possession of Lord Kitchener and has also been known as Kitchener's Island. Kitchener planned paths and irrigation patterns that made cultivation here possible. He also began a collection of tropical plants from around the world, which is now maintained by the Botanical Research Institute on the island.

LEFT:

Sir Seewoosagur Ramgoolam Botanical Garden, Port Louis, Mauritius
The oldest botanical garden in the Southern Hemisphere was established in 1770, when the island was a French colony and dominated by the French East India Company. The garden is named after the first prime minister of Mauritius and contains 80 tropical palm species.

ABOVE:

Seychelles Botanical Gardens, Mahé
Like Mauritius, the Seychelles were colonized by both the French and the British, and during this time the botanical gardens in Victoria, on the island of Mahé, were set up to trial crops with commercial potential. Today environmental education and sustainable tourism efforts are key activities of this lush space.

ALL PHOTOGRAPHS:
Babylonstoren, Western Cape, South Africa
On one of the oldest Cape-Dutch farms in the country,
now a hotel, French designer Patrice Taravella has created
a decorative productive garden of 15 rooms. These are set
against the imposing Simonsberg mountain and include a
prickly-pear maze, ponds planted with edible water lilies, and
thousands of clivias which bloom in spring.

ALL PHOTOGRAPHS:

**Kirstenbosch National Botanical Garden,
Western Cape, South Africa**

This truly unique garden spanning 528ha (1300 acres) on
the slopes of Table Mountain, Cape Town, is one of the
most important botanical gardens in the world for its role in
supporting the species-dense Fynbos biome. First inhabited
by indigenous Khoikhoi people, and then by European
settler-farmers, it was founded in 1913 and became part of
a UNESCO World Heritage Site in 2004. The Camphor Avenue
was planted in 1898. A new, 130m (425ft) long skywalk marks
the garden's centenary.

Meidan Emam, Isfahan, Iran
Open squares are fundamental to contemporary urban planning but one of the largest in the world dates from the early 17th century. Built by Abbas I the Great, this square is also known as Naqsh-e Jahan, translating as 'Image of the World'.

ALL PHOTOGRAPHS:

Bagh-e Eram, Shiraz, Iran
On the banks of the river Koshk lies a defining Islamic paradise garden, the name of which is the Persian word for heaven. The garden is thought to have been founded around the 12th century, and is one of nine Persian gardens in Iran awarded UNESCO World Heritage Site status for exemplifying the diversity of Islamic garden design. Water, in rills and fountains, is a central theme, as is abundant floristic planting.

Asia

From Japanese gardens tended in minute detail for centuries, to the most modern, subtropical conceptions in Singapore, Asia holds an extraordinary collection of gardens.

Much of the region's horticultural tradition emerged from China, where farming along the Yellow River and Yangtze River floodplains inevitably led to ornamental practices. Documents from as early as the 4th century BCE describe gardening for pleasure exclusively. Of the many horticultural landscapes in this vast and diverse country, the classical gardens in the city of Suzhou, all UNESCO World Heritage Sites, are among the best known.

Across the Yellow Sea and the Sea of Japan, the relative seclusion of the Japanese islands brought about a unique gardening tradition, although gardening practice has been influenced by neighbouring China and Korea. Gardens here are laden with symbolism, integral to Shinto beliefs and are at once about control and respect for landscape. Kenroku-en is one of the most compelling.

The Indian subcontinent has seen waves of rulers come and go, yet it was the Mughals who left an indelible horticultural mark here, beginning with Babur, who introduced the classic, quadrilateral Islamic garden or chahar bagh from Persia. Later, British colonialists sought to make their own impression on the jewel in the crown of the British Empire. At first this was through the commercially minded East India Company, but later Sir Edwin Lutyens, who earlier designed Surrey gardens with Gertrude Jekyll, was commissioned to lay out New Delhi, and Lord Curzon, Viceroy of India, refashioned the Taj Mahal to his taste. Our seemingly inexorably changing climate and the pressure on cities comes to the fore in densely populated Singapore where the Gardens by the Bay have been constructed with sustainability high on the agenda.

OPPOSITE:
Summer Palace, Beijing, China
With its layout based on Chinese mythology, the Summer Palace in Beijing comprises a sequence of connecting lakes, islands, hills, gardens and palaces. The largest feature is manmade Kunmig Lake, which covers 2.2 square km (0.85 square miles).

ALL PHOTOGRAPHS:

Humayun's Tomb, Delhi, India

Built for the second Mughal emperor Humayun in Delhi, this is the oldest of the Mughal garden-tombs on the Indian subcontinent. It was commissioned by the emperor's widow, Empress Bega Begum, in the mid-1500s, and designed by influential Mirak Mirza Ghiyas and Sayyid Muhammad, father and son. Inspired by the tastes of the first Mughal emperor, Babur, who had himself been moved by the gardens of Samarkand, the complex is a classic chahar bagh. Representing the afterlife in Islamic tradition, it a walled space divided into four by intersecting rills, with a central water source.

ALL PHOTOGRAPHS:
**Shalimar Gardens,
Jammu and Kashmir, India**
Emperor Akbar, the son of
Humayun, fell in love with
Kashmir when he visited
in the late 1500s. Around
Lake Dal in Srinagar, some
700 gardens were built, but
Shalimar Bagh is one of the
most enduring. Built in 1619
as an expression of love for
his wife Noor Jahan, it is
now a public park.

ALL PHOTOGRAPHS:

Taj Mahal, Uttar Pradesh, India

This incomparable complex in Agra was built between 1632 and 1653 by Emperor Shah Jahan, grandson of Akbar, for his wife, Mumtaz Mahal, who died in childbirth. The Taj Mahal was arranged in the Mughal style, and was intended as an intimate paradise garden planted with roses, narcissus, marigolds and jasmine. Shah Jahan's creation was remodelled in the early 20th century by Lord Curzon, Viceroy of India from 1898 to 1905, who was influenced by English parks. Under his direction, cypress trees were planted between the mausoleum and the gateway to the gardens.

ALL PHOTOGRAPHS:
Acharya Jagadish Chandra Bose Indian Botanic Garden, West Bengal, India

For centuries Kolkata was the apex of colonial trade with the East. The botanical garden here, on the banks of the great Hooghly river, was established in 1787 by an official in the East India Company. Like most botanical gardens of the British Empire, it was used for trialling plants with a commercial value. Key among these was tea – *Camellia sinensis* and *Camellia assamica* – the success of which precipitated India's substantial tea industry. Today the 109ha (269-acre) garden of lakes, long walks and vistas has a collection of some 12,000 plants, of which The Great Banyan, at 330m in circumference, is believed to be the largest tree in the world. The tree is supported with stilts.

Rock Garden of Chandigarh, Punjab and Haryana, India

It was a transport official of modest means, Nek Chand, who one day in the mid-1960s cleared a circle of jungle in his home city of Chandigargh, north India, to make a garden. Working by night to avoid detection, Chand gradually constructed a series of interlinking courtyards spanning several acres to house the sculpture he fashioned from discarded materials. It was a decade before he was discovered by city authorities and controversially given a salary and a small staff to continue his work. Today there are several thousand sculptures in the grounds, which are supported by the Nek Chand Foundation.

ALL PHOTOGRAPHS:
Summer Palace, Beijing, China
This perfectly preserved UNESCO World Heritage Site dates from the 12th century but took much of its current form under Qing Emperor Qianlong (1735–1796). Spread over almost 3km (2 miles), it epitomises the Chinese landscape aesthetic in its intention to balance human life with nature: 90 percent of the garden is designed for spiritual well-being. The Summer Palace has been damaged and restored under various regimes since it was first constructed, and is now a major tourist attraction.

Humble Administrator's Garden, Suzhou, China
The Hall of Distant Fragrances and the Pavilion in the Lotus Breeze are just two compelling features in the Humble Administrator's Garden, in Suzhou, west of Shanghai. Built in the classical and defining Suzhou style, the property dates from the 12th century but was developed in the 16th century by a retired government officer, the humble administrator. The historic garden is a UNESCO World Heritage Site.

ALL PHOTOGRAPHS:

Master-of-Nets Garden, Jiangsu, China

In Suzhou, his small but perfectly formed garden, a UNESCO World Heritage Site, is only an acre in size, but as in other classical gardens in this region, each element is exquisitely considered. It is a scholar's garden, with such elements as the Chapel of Accumulated Emptiness and the Pavilion Where the Moon Meets the Wind. Although it was first laid out in the 12th century by Shi Zhengzhi, the garden was redesigned by Song Zongyuan in 1785, with many features dating from this time. The garden is intended to express the simple life of a fisherman.

Kenroku-en, Ishikawa, Japan

With Koraku-en and Kairaku-en, Kenroku-en in Kanazawa is known as one of the Three Great Gardens of Japan. It was developed over 200 years from the 17th to the 19th centuries. The oldest building in the garden is a teahouse, built in 1774. The legs of a stone lantern resemble the shape of a *koto*, the Japanese national instrument. The lantern has become heraldic of the garden. In winter, ropes support tree branches to protect them from heavy snows in a technique known as *yukitsuri*.

140

ALL PHOTOGRAPHS:
Koishikawa Korakuen Garden, Tokyo, Japan
Few could have imagined how important a green lung for the city of Tokyo this park would become back when it was built in 1629 in the Edo period. One of the oldest parks in the city, it was instigated by Tokugawa Yorifusa and remained in this ruling family until 1869, when it was ceded to the Meiji government. It is at its best in spring and autumn, when it is coloured with blossom and turning leaves respectively.

ALL PHOTOGRAPHS:
ACROS building, Fukuoka City, Japan
Roof gardens and living walls are meaningful responses to climate change and habitat loss in dense cities, where they can also offer a pleasing design aesthetic. The ACROS Fukuoka Prefectural International Hall in Fukuoka City was at the forefront of green architecture when it was completed in 1994. Designed by Argentinian green architect Emilio Ambasz, it features an inclining wall of 15 planted terraces which are open to the public. Zig-zagging walkways lead to a roof garden.

Shisen-do temple, Kyoto, Japan
Ishikawa Jozan built Shisen-do as a mountain retreat or hermitage in 1641. The samurai-turned-poet sought retreat from the pressures of life and that same tranquil air remains in the garden today. It is from the hermitage that Jozan wrote the poetry in the Chinese style for which he became known. Azaleas and maples bring colour to the garden in spring and autumn; their forms contrast with the controlled aesthetic of clipped shrubs and a gravel garden.

Nong Nooch Tropical Garden, Pattaya City, Thailand

Spread over 200ha (500 acres), this tropical garden is one of the largest in Southeast Asia. At first it was intended the land would be given to a commercial plantation but upon seeing ornamental gardens abroad, the owners changed tack. Opened to the public as a tourist destination in 1980, today its extraordinary attractions include palm, orchid and cycad collections, a Thai topiary garden, French- and Italian-style gardens, and Stone Henge garden.

Singapore Botanic Gardens, Singapore

One of the world's most important botanical gardens, this UNESCO World Heritage Site was founded in 1882. Among the first plants trialled here was the Pará rubber tree (*Hevea brasiliensis*) and success spawned commercial plantations across the region. Described as the 'Kew of the East', the institution has maintained a notable orchid breeding programme since 1928, while the Herbarium houses around 750,000 specimens from the Malesian region. The gardens are an important green lung in the city.

Gardens by the Bay, Singapore
If the Singapore Botanic Gardens focus is on regional plants, the Gardens by the Bay take quite the opposite approach. Hundreds of thousands of plant species from around the world are assembled in this vast public garden covering over 100ha (247 acres). Domes, skywalks and cloud forests and the world's largest glass greenhouse may be found here. Opened in 2011, the gardens have a strong sustainability focus, with features such as photovoltaic cells contained within the garden's iconic Supertree Observatory.

Australasia and the Pacific

A panoply of influences, styles and intentions shape the gardens of this great region, which ranges from the rainforests of equatorial Indonesia to the icy glaciers of South Island, New Zealand.

In Bali, religious persuasions have led to water gardens offering peace and solitude, in spite being within range of an active volcano.

Across Australia, city founders established parks and gardens to cement an identity on a region, but now find that identity shifting as Australia becomes more international and the role of Aborigine people is acknowledged. Today botanic gardens strive to collect, protect and promote the extraordinary indigenous flora of this vast continent.

Research increasingly confirms what many have long known – which is that gardening can have a profound positive influence on mental health. In New South Wales, Wendy Whitely created a relative Eden from wasteland, and in doing so has overcome her own demons.

Other, intensely personal gardens are the result of creative vision and a direct response to landscape, whether that is farmland or snow-capped mountains.

OPPOSITE:
Tirta Gangga, Bali, Indonesia
This 1.2ha (3-acre) water garden in east Bali, was built to create a place of relaxation and holiness for residents and visitors. The name derives from the holy river Ganges, in India. Tirta Gangga has a look of great age but in fact dates only from 1948. With the active volcano of Mount Agung in the background, its three levels feature fountains and decorative ponds.

ALL PHOTOGRAPHS:
Chinese Garden of Friendship, New South Wales, Australia
To mark Australia's bicentennial celebrations, these gardens
in a goods yard in Darling Harbour, Sydney, were opened
in 1988. In a gesture of goodwill, the 1ha (2.47-acre)
gardens were initiated by the city's Chinese community,
and are designed in the *lingnan* style typical of the city of
Guangzhou. Plants include magnolias and abutilon, also
known as Chinese lantern.

ALL PHOTOGRAPHS:

Wendy's Secret Garden,
New South Wales, Australia
On the north shore of Sydney
Harbour, Wendy Whiteley
began to garden a tract of
abandoned public land after
overcoming heroin addiction
and the death of her husband
and daughter. The sloping
site has views of the city
skyline and planting is lush
with palms and native flora.

ALL PHOTOGRAPHS:
Adelaide Botanical Gardens, South Australia, Australia
In this state capital, the botanic gardens and the associated state herbarium work to contribute to sustainability and biodiversity with living, cultural and preserved collections. The 51ha (126-acre) garden was opened in 1857 in response to pressure to establish a public garden in the city. The Bicentennial Conservatory is one of the largest in the Southern Hemisphere.

ALL PHOTOGRAPHS:

Royal Botanic Gardens, Victoria, Australia
On the banks of the Yarra river, Melbourne, with lawns, lakes and garden beds, this public garden houses over two dozen living plant collections. The visitor can find collections of eucalypts, cycads, ferns and plants from New Zealand, New Caledonia, Southern Africa and South China. A second site in Cranbourne features a striking, contemporary dry garden planted with around 1,700 plant types from southeast Australia.

BOTH PHOTOGRAPHS::
Brisbane Botanic Gardens, Queensland, Australia
At the foot of Mount Coot-tha, these gardens in subtropical
Brisbane hold significant collections of rainforest plants. The
56ha (138-acre) garden was opened in 1976, and attractions
include fern and bonsai houses and a Japanese garden. There are
also plant collections from the Pacific Islands around Australia
and a geodesic dome housing tropical specimens.

Pukekura Park, Taranaki, New Zealand
Originally swamp or wetland, this popular public space in New Plymouth was opened in 1876. It covers 52ha (128 acres), and includes gardens and recreational areas. The Queen Elizabeth II Fountain was built in 1955 to mark a Royal visit to this key member of the British Commonwealth. Other features are Japanese and Chinese Gardens and a water lily lake.

ALL PHOTOGRAPHS & OVERLEAF:
Stonefields, Victoria, Australia
Paul Bangay is one of Australia's best-known garden designers and his property Stonefields, near Daylesford, reflects a lifetime of gardening. Tucked between some of Victoria's premier wine estates, this large farm bears Italian influences with formal hedges and topiary providing a sense of enclosure. The garden contains such classic elements as a rose parterre, reflective pond and a rill, which runs the length of the space.

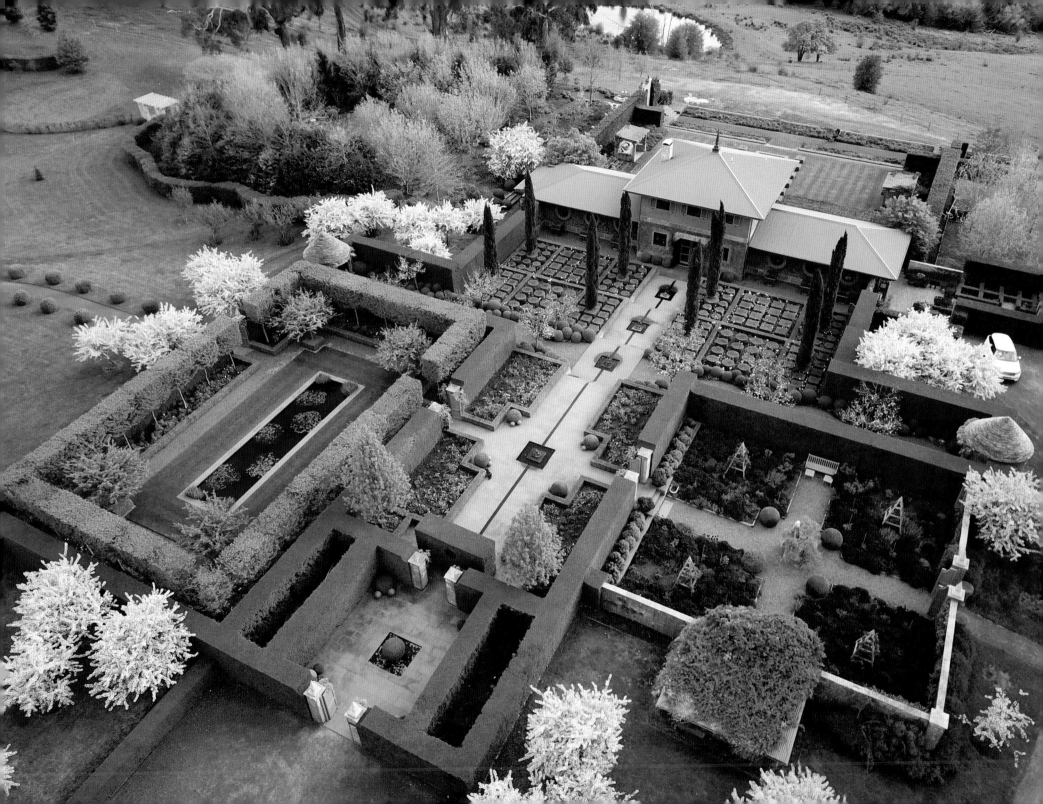

ALL PHOTOGRAPHS:

**Flaxmere Garden,
Canterbury, New Zealand**
This garden on a sheep
farm in North Canterbury,
has been developed over 50
years by Penny and John
Zino. With Mount Tekoa
in the distance, vistas are
key here – as is water,
which is contained in five
ponds across the property.
Planting includes many
native New Zealand species
which are combined with
rhododendrons and roses.
A woodland area comes to
the fore in autumn.

North and South America

From the great, sweeping, temperate landscapes of North America to the richly biodiverse latitudes of Central America and down to the subtropical and tropical regions of South America, these two continents hold an awe-inspiring range of horticultural feats.

Some, like the many post-war Japanese gardens in the United States, have been built to encourage good relations between communities. Others are expressions of the new-found wealth of their owners, who might have grown rich from pharmaceuticals or mining at the turn of the last century. In these gardens nothing but the finest would do. Gardens have also always been an outlet for creativity, providing a splendid canvas on which to effect one's imaginings. Edward James and Edith Wharton knew this well.

As we progress into the 21st century, thoughts turn to the First Nations, resilience, sustainability and biodiversity. Gardens with these themes in mind acknowledge the richness of our natural heritage and the profound influence it has on our quality of life.

The futuristic Seattle Spheres present a biophilic working space that may well become common place in the near future. Meanwhile abandoned railway lines and empty city spaces are planted for humans and urban wildlife alike.

OPPOSITE:
Butchart Gardens, British Columbia, Canada
When Jennie Butchart wondered what to do with a disused limestone quarry on the property she and her husband, Robert, owned outside Victoria in 1904, she turned it into a densely planted sunken garden.

ALL PHOTOGRAPHS:

Hatley Castle, British Columbia, Canada

The Edwardian mansion of one of British Columbia's most prominent businessmen, James Dunmuir, was built in 1908 on Vancouver Island. Garden designers Franklin Brett and George D. Hall laid out the property in English country house style, and included Victorian design elements to make the garden appear older – and more prestigious – than it was. Today herbaceous borders, a rose garden, Italian garden and a Japanese garden are key attractions.

177

ALL PHOTOGRAPHS:

Montreal Botanical Garden, Quebec, Canada
Some 21,000 different plants are contained in the Montreal Botanical Garden founded in 1931. The orchid genus *Teuscheria*, native to Central America, was named after the first curator of the garden, Henry Teuscher. First Nations, Chinese and Japanese gardens run alongside 10 greenhouses, a large lake and traditional rose, perennial and shrub gardens. In 2013 the garden hosted the international living sculpture exhibition *Mosaïcultures Internationales* (bottom left and right).

OVERLEAF:

Butchart Gardens, British Columbia, Canada
Jennie Butchart's vision for a disused lime quarry was developed over several generations, beginning in 1904. Butchart's rose garden, Italian garden and Japanese garden remain. In 2004, two Totem Poles were dedicated in the garden to mark the centenary of the garden and the cultural heritage of First Nations in the area.

ALL PHOTOGRAPHS:
Van Dusen Botanical Garden, British Columbia, Canada
It is difficult to miss the maze of 3,000 planted cedars (*Thuja occidentalis* 'Fastigiata') in the VanDusen Botanical Garden towards the south of the Vancouver. A hexagonal Korean pavilion was donated to the garden from the Korean people – it is surrounded by the Cypress Pond. Attached to the garden is the Bloedel Conservatory, which has a special focus on palms and tropical plants.

ALL PHOTOGRAPHS:

The Mount, Massachusetts, USA

Novelist Edith Wharton designed and built The Mount in 1902. The first woman to win a Pulitzer prize for her novel *The Age of Innocence* (1920), she documented the wealthy New York life of which she was a part. Yet The Mount was where, with her niece Beatrix Farrand, she turned her hand to gardening. The elegant New England garden is a series of outdoor rooms that includes a sunken Italian garden, gravel promenades and a rock garden.

ALL PHOTOGRAPHS:
Dumbarton Oaks, Washington, D.C., USA
Born in 1872, Beatrix Farrand designed hundreds of upper-class gardens on the US coasts, including spaces at the New York Botanical Garden and The White House, but at Dumbarton Oaks she excelled. One of her few surviving works, it was owned by Robert and Mildred Bliss, who commissioned her to create a mix of formal and informal bedding arrangements drawing from Arts and Crafts, and classic English and Italian elements. The collaboration began in 1921 and ended nearly 30 years later. Farrand died in seclusion in Maine in 1959. Dumbarton Oaks is now a Harvard University humanities research institute, and the gardens remain open to view.

ALL PHOTOGRAPHS
AND OVERLEAF:
Atlanta Botanical Garden, Georgia, USA
Comparatively new in botanical garden terms, the Atlanta Botanical Garden opened in 1976 upon the petition of local residents. The garden's mission is to aid botanical education, conservation, research and enjoyment. It regularly hosts popular exhibitions from the likes of glass sculptor Dale Chihuly, whose fantastical creations have been shown around the world. In 2010 the garden was expanded and modernised.

ABOVE:

Chicago Botanic Garden, Illinois, USA
This popular tourist attraction spanning 156ha (385 acres)
within the Cook Country Forest Preserve was opened in 1972.
It is divided into four zones reflecting local natural habitat:
woods, prairie, riparian landscape and lakes and shores. A
native plant garden and sensory garden are among the more
contemporary attractions here.

RIGHT:

Garfield Park Conservatory, Illinois, USA
One of the largest conservatories in the United States,
with nearly a hectare under glass, this notable Chicago
conservatory dates to the 19th century. The largest room in
the conservatory is the Palm House, which at 65ft high and
90ft wide accommodates 70 palms from around the world.
The glasshouses and the surrounding park are listed on the
National Register of Historic Places.

Chanticleer, Philadelphia, USA
On the outskirts of Philadelphia, Chanticleer dates from the early 1900s and was built by Adolph and Christine Rosengarten, who had a pharmaceuticals business. Few expenses were spared in its construction, leading the Rosengartens to name their home after the property in Thackeray's novel *The Newcomes*, which was 'mortgaged up to the very castle windows'. Some 14 staff now manage Chanticleer, which is part of the Chanticlere Foundation and open to the public. Productive gardens, woodland, ponds, a gravel garden, terraces and a flowery lawn feature.

ALL PHOTOGRAPHS:
Fairchild Tropical Botanic Garden, Florida, USA
Just south of Miami, this botanic garden spread over 34ha
(84 acres), conducts important research into biodiversity and
is also the home of the American Orchid Society. It is named
after plant hunter-explorer David Fairchild, who introduced
thousands of plants to the United States, not least certain
bamboos, mangoes and dates.

ALL PHOTOGRAPHS:

Golden Gate Park, California, USA
In San Francisco, this memorable park in the centre of the city
is larger but similar in design and function to Central Park
in Manhattan. Gardens here comprise meadows, groves and
lakes, while the infamous-but-loved Hippie Hill has been a site
of counterculture since the 1960s.

Huntington Library and Gardens, California, USA
Dry-climate plants and native species are a hallmark of the California Garden here. It is one of 16 themed gardens, including a Japanese garden, at this popular location in San Marino outside Los Angeles. The Desert Garden holds one of the world's largest collections of cacti and succulents. Research, workshops and lectures are integral to this institution.

ALL PHOTOGRAPHS:

Longwood Gardens, Pennsylvania, USA
The extraordinary grounds at Longwood Gardens draw visitors from around the world. This well-regarded botanical garden is one of the finest in the United States and it is an important place of learning and research for horticulturalists and botanists. The Longwood Garden plant collection contains over 9,000 species and varieties and dates to 1798.

PREVIOUS PAGES:
Portland Japanese Garden, Oregon, USA
With a view of the city of Portland, this considered West Coast garden was borne of the desire to build relations between Oregon and Japan in the 1950s, post World War II – as were many other Japanese gardens around the United States. The garden opened to the public formally in 1967 although the garden continues to evolve, with development taking place as recently as 2017.

OPPOSITE AND RIGHT:
US Botanical Garden, Washington, D.C., USA
This historic garden is housed within the grounds of the United States Capitol. Initiated by George Washington 200 years ago, it can claim to be the oldest continuously operating botanic garden in the United States. Its reported purpose is to promote botanical knowledge, present displays of plants to Congress and the public and foster sustainability and plant conservation.

ALL PHOTOGRAPHS:

The Highline, New York City, USA

From a disused railway line in New York City's
Meatpacking District has emerged one of the most
compelling gardens in the world. The Highline, designed
by master of the New Perennial movement Piet Oudolf, is a
sinuous, 2.3km (1.44-mile) long elevated park with planting
designed for all seasons of the year. It is maintained and
operated by the Friends of the Highline.

LEFT:

Lurie Gardens Millennium Park, Illinois, USA
The New Perennial planting style, which has come to define a section of horticulture in the first quarter of the 21st century, is triumphant in the Lurie Gardens in Chicago. Designer Piet Oudolf worked with a team of designers to create a 'four-season garden' with emphasis on wildlife, sustainability and enjoyment. A spring bulb display is deftly arranged by eminent Dutch designer Jaqueline van der Kloet.

RIGHT:

Lurie Gardens Millennium Park, Illinois, USA
The gardens are situated on the roof of a parking garage, and have a minimum soil depth of 45cm (18in) in places. Many plant species, such as those in the *Echinacea* genus (pictured), are prairie natives and are a magnate for butterflies, birds and other urban wildlife.

ALL PHOTOGRAPHS:
**Seattle Spheres,
Washington, USA**
Establishing a direct link to nature is integral to Seattle Spheres, the futuristic-looking office space used by Amazon. Over 40,000 plants grow within the glass-domed building, specifically forming green or living walls. The structure is a reflection of biophilic design, which is gaining traction in buildings around the world, from hospitals and classrooms to office spaces.

ALL PHOTOGRAPHS:

Hunte's Botanical Gardens, Barbados
Intended to be a recreation of a Caribbean forest, Hunte's Botanical Gardens, situated on a former sugar plantation in St Joseph, was begun by one Anthony Hunte in the 1950s. Today paths meander through lush tropical planting complete with the vibrant colours and forms associated with the region.

ALL PHOTOGRAPHS:

Vallarta Botanical Gardens, Jalisco, Mexico

Native Mexican plants thrive in this notable botanical garden in Puerto Vallato on the west coast of Mexico. The intention of this garden is to showcase the great variety of Mexican plant species. Additional attractions include an orchid collection and viewing trails. The gardens are curated by Robert Price, who is also founder of the garden.

ALL PHOTOGRAPHS:

**Jardín Escultórico Edward James, Las Pozas,
San Luis Potosi, Mexico**

Edward James was an avid collector of Surrealist art. Having washed up in the small Mexican town of Xilita in the 1940s, he developed one of the most remarkable Surrealist gardens in the world. Arches, columns and Escher-like stairs define this garden which is thick with Mexican vegetation. In a quest to create an everlasting garden, James created numerous sculptures in botanical forms. James died in 1984 whereupon the garden was opened to the public.

OPPOSITE (BOTH PHOTOGRAPHS):
**Sítio Roberto Burle Marx,
Rio de Janeiro, Brazil**
This UNESCO World
Heritage Site on the outskirts
of Rio de Janeiro houses a
considerable collection of
tropical and subtropical
plants. The former home of
Brazilian landscape architect
Roberto Burle Marx, it was
built over 40 years to create a
"living work of art" drawing
on his modernist ideas. Burle
Marx was inspired by the
Modern Art movement and
Portuguese and Brazilian folk
traditions.

RIGHT:
**Jardim Botânico Rio
de Janeiro, Brazil**
Within sight of the city's
famous Christ the Redeemer
statue, this botanic garden
was founded in 1808 by King
John VI of Portugal. It houses
a noteworthy collection of
tropical plants and highlights
the diversity of Brazilian
flora. Like other botanical
gardens, it began as a place
to trial commercial crops, in
this case nutmeg, pepper and
cinnamon. The garden has
an important research facility
attached to it.

ALL PHOTOGRAPHS:

Jardín Japonés, Buenos Aires, Argentina
One of the largest Japanese gardens outside Japan in the world, this garden is managed by the Japanese Argentine Cultural Foundation. Construction was completed in 1967, and the public space is valued for cultivating links between the two countries. Features include bonsai, a lake and various Japanese plant species.

Picture Credits